State of

Reverie

Desiree M. Humphrey

Dedication

To my family and friends who have been positive and
supportive in my many endeavors

A special thanks to my two editors: Mom & Cousin Brooke

Table of Content   Page

Super Eclipse Moon

Eyes zoned in on the night sky

Gazing upon the majestic moon

The excitement of the disappearing act puts you in a state of

awe

I feel what is not seen,

I see what is not there

Red darkness engulfs its radiance,

While the earth cast its ominous shadow across the angelic

sphere

As darkness slowly ensues,

A celebration commences

Awaiting the reappearance of the omniscient moon,

I dance in anticipation

Its full luminescence blankets the night sky with lunar rays

I feel the power,

The power of the Super Eclipse Moon

Ghost

Top hat man walking down the street

Where will you go?

Who will you meet?

A gentleman with pride held high

You feel warmth of the sun

I feel rays of moonlight

Rebirth in a Dream

Through the window of dreams,
I see her lying in the street
Motionless, death has become her
As I look upon her in colorful attire and long dark hair,
I feel indifferent
No fear, No sorrow, No pain
Unchained from her troubles that haunted her present
She is no longer weighed down by her pernicious past,
But released into her beatific future
She is I
I see beauty in death
Dead in the street,
She is the beginning of my newly awakened life

Blue and Charlotte

A soundless wind carries essence of peace
Magnetic hearts fly together as one
Bashfully resting on a brick partition
Drawing closer to each other eager for love
Grooming wings of flight,
Playful touches and caressing beaks
A flightless mount, binding soft earthly feathers
Symbol of peace and love embodied by two brown doves

Chip the Mockingbird

Oh Mockingbird, how you sing so lovely at three in the morning

Oh Mockingbird, you will not rest till your voice is heard

Day and night you play your harmonious tune

Stationary in your domain, you call out timelessly

Determined little bird, do you ever sleep?

I hear your chirp loud and clear

Your message I receive,

As you sing "Never stop doing what you love to do, not even at three"

Rainbow of the Night

Rainbow of the night

Your colors shine so bright

Surrounding the full moon

Cradling its shape not a moment too soon

An aberrant order of vibrant hues

The clouds move with alacrity to show a new view

Yellow, red, purple, blue, and green

The rainbow of the night in spender and sheen

The diaphanous clouds glide across the moonlight

I hope once again I can gaze upon the rainbow of the night

Returning Soulmate

You returned to me like a red blazing tempest
My body reacts with celerity ardor
You direct me to a path of illusory dreams lost long ago
A familiar intoxicating scent keeps me blind to the illusion
you masterfully conjured
You offer a taste of brown elixir,
To temporarily efface my wits

The sun rises and I awaken from your spell
As I abscond by morning light,
Your true nature clearly shows
You surround yourself with counterfeits,
Hiding behind your nugatory words
Unable to find your true worth in this lifetime

He, broken and wounded,
My heart breaks for the man I once loved in a previous life
Our paths may have crossed once again,
Yet fate points us to two different roads
I still hold hope that you find your way,
Becoming the great man I knew a lifetime ago

Black Circle

Coming to a sacred place to behold
I sit in a marked sphere
While meditating a vison unfolds

Vibrations emerge from the ground up
A trance I am in, my third eye fills its cup
Lush green forest and trees for miles
An unusual wooden tower, erect all the while
Fast forward to an arduous trail in the desert
Sadness in her eyes with a swarm of sorrow in an unbearable
measure

I waken, empathic tears flowing down
The world seen grey, no color to be found
An honor of sight from a distant native being
A present of a shaman warrior, felt but never seen

Skepta

Listening to "Underdog Sycosis"
Awakened from a dark abyss
Embedding zeal that was lost in the depts of a labyrinth
within my soul
Able to understand myself through Joseph's words
Joyful tears stream down my face

A long lost relatable message immerges from the lips of a
lyricist
A weight lifted
A spark reignited
I proclaim my truth again
No longer shall the turmoil skim the surface of my thought
Eyes and ears kissed by an MC
Life was returned to me

21st Century Medusa

Her essence calls to you
A yearning ripens from your loins
Her smile weakens your heart
Her voice soft and seductive,
Muting warnings and cautions in your head

Her body is the serpent that hypnotize
Alluring the strongest of men
Your senses become perturbed
You only feel desire
When she wants you,
Be vigilant!
For you are no longer the hunter,
But become her prey

She knows her power is great,
Wheeling it when her appetite grows
Your tactics and strategies are useless,
For she pierces through your defenses with a passionate touch
Turning lions, bulls, and dragons of men into stone

Gaze upon her eyes and you convert as her acolyte
Forever silent and devoted
Beware of the 21st Century Medusa

21st Century Medusa

Amy's Mr. Magic

Green the color of my leaf
Beneficial to all,
Consumed by some
Historically revered by society,
You are something supernatural

Coming straight from mother earth,
You provide an array of benefits
Opening our eyes to what we ignore to see
Yes it is used and yes it is abused
But my sticky friend gives clarity,
And truth beyond what my diluted conscience can provide

Happiness is brought in
Worries is exhaled out
You can choose to enhance your ability,
Or lose yourself in ignorant temporary bliss
This sweet meat can devour your presents in the world
A dependency can be installed

Understanding your capability within a small nugget
A tool used to its fullest potential
Slip into a daze with haze
Green is the color of my leaf
Gray is the color of no more

Aphrodite's Visit Home

Returning home,

Welcomed with an oceanic embrace

Aphrodite reunited with the sea

Clear watered carpet trimmed with seafoam rolled out for the

Goddess of love

A crown and adornments of seaweed and shells placed at her

feet

Seated upon a sandy throne,

A playful dance performed by enchanting waves of blue

Emerging energies,

Cleansing and renewing her soul

A short journey back home,

Nearing its bitter sweet end

A gift of love,

A token of remembrance

She returns to her mortal state,

And heads back to foreign land,

Awaiting the day to return to the sea

Missing her love, her life, her home

Caged Lioness

Trapped like an animal in a cage

Lost and frustrated in this social maze

Nowhere to turn to

Not left, Not right

Feeling there is no end in sight

Desire burning to be free

Struggling the fight within

Wanting to just be

Hopelessness in this never ending war

The lioness inside me yearning to break free and roar

**Caged
Lioness**

Thank You

Thank you for relinquishing me from your friendship
Thank you for showing me your maligned true self
I was blinded by the faint goodness harbored in your heart,
Only to be thrown in the path of your avaricious nature

Thank you for the lesson you have taught me
You disguise your hidden form with laughter and pleasantries
Thank you, for now I have abdicated listening to your unjust
one sided complaints

Thank you for no longer dumping your negativity upon me
The charm which you have fooled me with time and time
again lost its luster
Thank you, for I no longer have to empathize with you

Thank you for showing me your childish tantrums,
Reinforcing my feelings to repel from you
For now I feel more at peace,
When no words are spoken between us

The Question

Playful innocence appears in bronzed sentient forms

Catching me off guard

As I visualize my habitual responses,

They are inquisitive by my actions and reactions

I realize my passive ways

Stimulated with a question,

Eyes piercing thought my soul

Contemplating my answer in a conscience state

The important of self and the intuitive significance of the
universe as a whole

Figuring out my disconnection on the surface of societal life

Battling to understand my sensitive sensors to the world
around me

Through sleeping thoughts and awaken sight

My dreams become a second self though which I can confide

Snow Babies

Loving mother, loving wife and friend
Her kindness and generosity extended to no end
A kiss on the cheek puts a smile on her face
With opening arms, a grandmother's embrace

Her will was strong, her stamina was might
From her very last breath she gave one heck of a fight
An ageless beauty, Aphrodite would envy
Many knew her as Claire, but she was mother to many

Zipping through the aisles on her electric chariot with speed
Always willing to help others, a woman of good deeds
Painting snow babies with glitter on her face
Leveling up in Candy Crush with such dire haste

Farwell loving Claire, we will keep you in our hearts
Cherishing the memories with which we'll never part

Lucid Dream II

Like a beacon in the night, the aquatic membranes of lovers
floats within her dreams
As Mercury descends upon her new form,
He delivers a clairvoyant message from a devotee
Unknowing its roots, she decipher the feelings into verses of
poetry
Deeply hidden in the depts of her unknown desire, she feels
him in the form of tranquility

He strolls by her window as a phantom in the night,
Disguised as a top hatted gentleman
Centuries of roaming between realms of the living and dead,
Relentless determination to let her know his truth

A crescent embrace, feeling the warmth of love which time
never erased
Guided by Hermes to where her hearts locked away,
Placing a crystal rose upon her neck and leads her to sea

Twinkled light in the dark, his presents felt to be known
Waves in and out of consciousness, filtering a single thought
in reverie
Amnesia in this life, delicately removed to reveal
Glimpses of the past that illustrates the story of soul mates

Lace on her skin, passionate grasp of the arm

His missed opportunity of lyrics unable to be express
She sees her heart lost at the bottom of the sea

She questions the sights, trying to make since of it all
Pictured in his place of happiness, he expresses sadness and
sorrow
Finally she connects the dots, his message rings clear in her
ear

With his feels known, he is able to move on
Her heart now freed, unlocked by his words
The timing was wrong but the souls were right
Now both are unbound, able to meet each other again in this
present

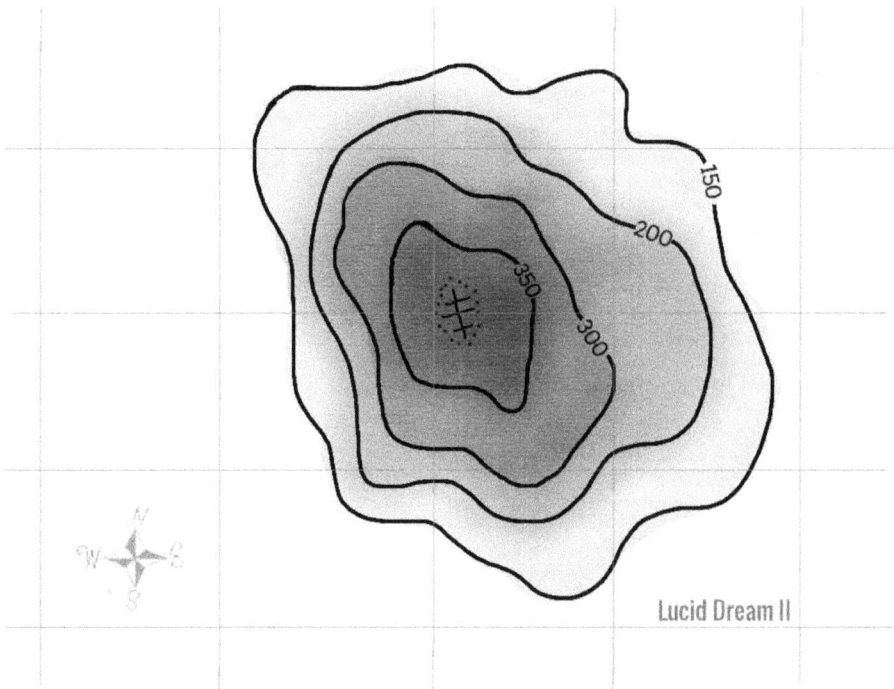

Lucid Dream II

Déjà vu

An aura of light shines around both of you
Remembering, reminiscing scenes from the past
A reconnection of my departed loved ones
Linking the points of my life with your guidance
A discovery awakened by your presence

Mythology, psychology, and anthropology hold root to my
conscience
Creativity, imagination, and curiosity hold root to my
subconscious
A gift you knew I had that stem from heritage
From the voodoo swampland to the shaman forest
I am what I am

Embrace your true inner self you say
Enhance your emotions
Reflect on the past,
And dig deeper into thought
See life for what it is, as you have nothing to fear
We will help guide, for we are forever with you

We are Human

Read between the lines of my voice,

For I am only man

Society deals me my formula,

Shaping me from a plastic mold

Show no emotion and show no signs of weakness

For I am only man

Teach our sons not to cry

Display strength by aggression

Teach our daughter to decipher our words,

To understand what I cannot express

Continue this cycle taught at youth,

For I am only man

Hear my words that I sing to you,

For I am woman

Patience, understanding, love and compassion make my

formula

I break the mold from which I was produced

I exude emotion and wear badges of tears proudly,

For I am woman

Teach my fathers, brothers, sons, and lovers,

Discard your mold because you are man

Communicate your emotions

No longer shall woman need to decrypt your code

Express it,

For we are all human

Grandfriend

Untypical fairy godfather, I call Grandfriend
Spiritually connected, you speak my truth
When in my thoughts, a call from you arrives
In need of guidance and understanding,
You enlighten my path
In a dark world you encourage stamina, humility and
contemplation
Twisted as he claims to be,
But wise beyond my years
I see a spiritual guide with sincere kindness in his heart
Fate intertwine our souls,
For he know me sometimes better than I know myself
A friendship incomparable to any wealth
I never need fear when I'm in good company

Dark Happiness

I feel most at peace when life is at its slumber
The moon arises
Beaming gently upon the sleeping earth
The crescent's rays light up the sparkled nocturnal sky
I feel the stillness
Calmness is what I hear
Serene is the nigh

Turquoise Stone Egg

She finds herself in sanctuary
At a time of lost and vulnerability,
This hibernating egg slowly hatches to show its beauty
Eyes that sparkle in the darkness of night,
Looks towards the sky ready for discovery
Unforeseen forces make the flight arduous
Impermanent chains, cages and traps almost devour the
creature on her path
She still strides forward,
Heading in the right direction on the journey of fate
Striving to reach her goal,
Emancipation

Wish for True Love

A falling star, a flash of light
A stream of glitter in the night
Make a wish, let your heart be true
A will of thought becomes anew
Flying across the deep above
Hoping, dreaming, waiting for her wish of true love

Rare Flower

Rare Flowers

Intellect stems from the seeds of knowledge

Curiosity feeds the sprout which grows in the nutrient soil

Egotistical foliage irritate these delicate plants like a perpetual
rash,

Trying to uproot and shadow truth

Devious cultivators attempt to pluck the innocents from the
earth,

Leaving the decaying shrubbery of society left behind to taint
the dirt

Still these floral pink warriors fight to reach sun rays of love,

Which feeds the roots of their spiritual growth

Springing forth to bloom,

Fragrancing the air with peace, love, and tranquility

Swords and Daggers

Running out of patience, in a hurry to go nowhere

I call you out, and you throw daggers

Once I stood in the way of these daggers

Yesterday I burdened the pain,

Today I step aside

For these daggers you throw are pieces from the sword you

penetrate yourself

You teach me lessons from the agony you harbor

Your inner turmoil is far more painful than the daggers you

throw

Trouble you are

Trouble I don't have to be

Let go and release those knives

Understand this lesson

Never stab yourself with a sword and throw daggers at others

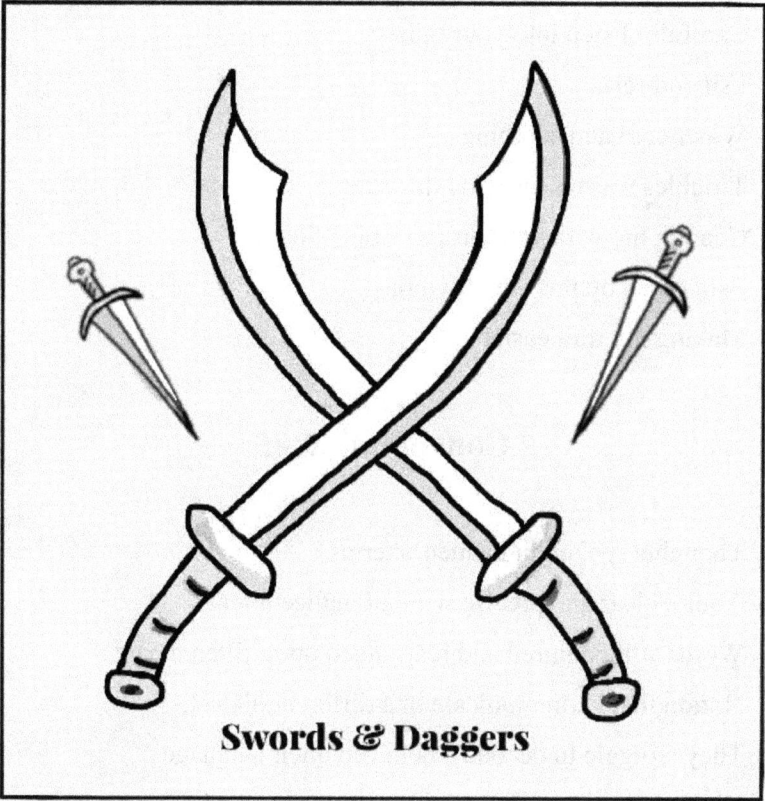

Swords & Daggers

Sprained Ankle

Navigated to the stream, it summons me

Inviting me into its enticing ripples

The flow hypnotizes my wounded senses

Carefully I step into your falls

I sit and relax

Water cool and soothing

Troubles washes away by the river

Coating me with your drops of blue liquid

Pain eased by the water nymph

Making my trail easier

Conversation #5

Thoughts spoken in laymen's terms

Audio, clear and precise without malice intent

Words still conjured and rearranged upon filtered ears

Notion that I communicate in a different dialect,

They struggle to decode a believed alien language

Hindering my vociferous nature,

Muting my passion within

A fortress erects in my emotions

Blocking those that refuse to listen

Silently at work, my frustrations released

Yet I feel the harbored animosity aimed at me,

From those whose second chances have run out

Star Gazing

Night falls, darkness creeps in
Looking up to the azure universe,
Seeing crystal seeds twinkling down
Beyond our thoughts, dreams, and wishes,
Two majestic stars shoot across the vast blanket of space
Time dissipates, when lost in the pool of the unknown
Marvel at the beauty,
Which has diminished in the eyes of our past
Mapping the dots,
Creating giants from legendary myth
Silent in its mist yet vivacious with grandeur
A free show of discovery gazing at the stars

Element of Water

Following in no direction, my compass points to thee
I dream of you often, crystal blue sea
You call to me by night; I yearn for you by day
Streaming through my dreams, showing me the way
Flowing with the moon, harboring creatures of the deep
You know no bounds to the lessons you may teach
Touched by fate, your sirens sing of peace
Voices drifting in the wind, a summon of release
Constantly in my head, flowing through my mind
The element of water is never far behind

Lucid Dream III

Sailing by in different boats,

To each own wind we are afloat

Guided by the books of our lives unfolding as we go,

Feeling the waves of life sway to and fro

Following institution,

Letting the universe speak with signs

Currents moving to destinations where energies combined

Our boats may cross paths,

Our sails could pass and meet

Drifting together in the vastness to our own oceanic beat

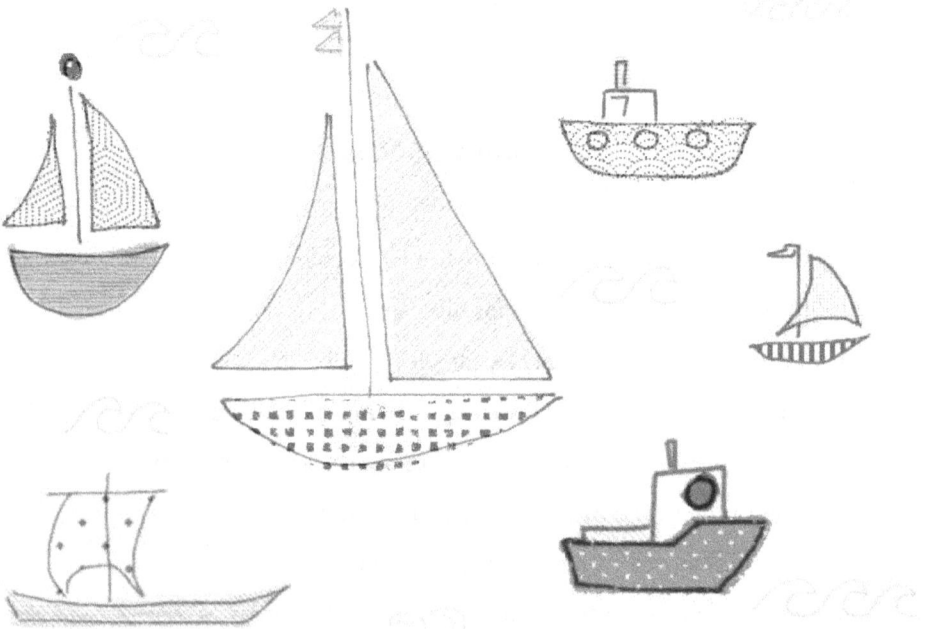

Lucid Dream III

Jumbled Speech

My thoughts are fast

An encyclopedia of stimulating material

Sifting through vast pages of knowledge

The wheels in my mind turn at a rapid pace,

Filtering the mental notes accumulated in daily life,

Most of which go unnoticed and unseen by most

My voice is slow

Unable to navigate quickly to find the right words

In speech, words collide in a chaos of thought

A rush of verses stumbles from my lips,

Spilling on ordinary ears

Softly spoken to mask the scatter of words

Dialog to slow for the world

Data too fast for the absent minded

Unable to normalize

I stay silent

Becoming a master listener

The lost art of thoughtful tongue

Taught to me by a master of PHD's

Highly intellectual being

Our conversation progressed at a tortoise speed

Collecting ideas and removing redundant fillers

Words elegantly flow to convey a precise train of though

Familiar Light

Conformity

Justifications need by my actions

Feeling like a fixture in this monetary cult

Opinions voiced, questions asked

Wondering what I feel, thinks, wear, and eat is acceptable

I say, "SCREW SOCIETY",

With its judgmental hypocrisy

Stained in my head like oil on silk

I tried to conform to what is normal and expected

Hidden within the depths of my bosom,

Rebellion steeps out

Shedding its skin to reveal a unique creature

Forever changing, forever evolving

Learning that the only justification needed is from within

Familiar Light

Your aura resonates in the corner of my eye

Turning my head I look to your presences

Reflection of the past within present time

Objects acquired embody your space

Warming my heart

Leading to reflections and self-revolution, I think of you

Impregnated creativity and curiosity to a naïve descendant

Tonight things start to come together

Reveling a greater purpose, still yet to be fully discovered

Round 2

Round two, let's see what you can do
My expectations are low
Yet my emotions are high
Motivation and challenge ignited
Slowly developed determinations,
Not for you but for me
A better self I will present to you
You will see
The expectations for myself are high
My approval and acceptance of you are low
Round two, let's see that you can do

Urban Jungle

Lost will, will to fight
The urban jungle drains my strength
Wearing down my temple
Sucking the energy like a leech
Freedom is what I desire,
Stillness is hard to come by in this concrete place
Destiny just beyond my reach
I have to take my freedom back
Muster up all of my strength to release myself
For if I do not change, I will become a slave to this urban
jungle

Wrong Man/Right Man

A fantasy of a man falsely imagined
The showmanship cleverly devised
An ardent yearning slowly fades,
Transferring into feelings of disappointment
The vail across her eyes sheds with every encounter

Waiting the day she encounters a man beyond her fantasy
More complex than ever imagined
With sight clear and true, loves comes to her
He is no magician but a captain of love
Not wanting to deceive and mystify,
He has zeal to possess her heart and all its glory

Beyond
the
Moon

Beyond the Moon

Looking to the sky,
Dazzled by the midnight canvas
What lies beyond the moon I wonder?

The stars roar with fire
Life survives in its mist
A galaxy yet unknown
An empire perhaps or space patrol?
Creatures unknown to our imagination
What lies beyond the moon I wonder?

My mind full of endless possibilities
My mind curious to know
Never to old to dream
Eyes gazing past the lunar rock
What lies beyond the moon I wonder?

Sirens of the Sea

Her voice is soothing,

Her eyes lure you close

Hypnotized to revile your darkest secret within

Like a siren, her song puts you at ease

Her beauty all alluring

Her melody you hear

Enraptured in her glory,

Your death will come near

Tell her your inner thoughts

For the truth will set you free

"Come closer" she chimes, like a whisper in the wind

"Free yourself and become one of me"

Physiognomist

Trained master of physiognomy

Seeing behind the mask commonly purchased by the mass

Facial expressions, actions, and tones giveaway true nature

Unable to lie, manipulate and disguise the truth

Eyes of a physiognomist pierce through the deceptions,

Reading the souls and hearts of others

Blessed and cursed with this gift,

Isolation and frustration burden the shoulders of the few

Striding forward, taking refuge with a mentor

Finally able to interact freely amongst a similar kind

Meant For

Your arms are meant to embrace me
My hands are meant to hold you face
Your mouth is meant to kiss my breast
My tongue is meant to caress your lips
Your eyes are meant to look upon mine
My smile is meant to warm you
Your heart is meant for me
My heart is meant for you
Come to me,
I am waiting for you

Patience

Patience I hear, softly ring like a toll bell
Stillness flowing in the faint breeze
The fast pace life pulls me
Dragging me across the mud
Keeping my heart at a unsettling beat
Trying to free myself from the wheels of so called "life"
To live at peace within myself and the universe
Kicking and screaming to be understood
Unchain me from the whirlwind of this nation
Take control of this vicissitude of my life
Patience I hear,
Letting stillness fill me to completion

Man in the Designer Suit

Something about you I can't understand

You fuel a dim fire inside me to a colossal ardent blaze

My heart becomes tempestuous

Desires grow quickly

Why now? Why you?

You inspire me, you enrage me

A yin and yang of emotions

Passion and disgust

Happiness and sorrow

Yet your face is always a mystery,

Like my unjust stirring for you

Dancing Star

Dazed behind a screen, I notice you

Sending out flickers of light

Curiously I listen

Dancing with fury, flickering to your own beat

I feel you

The magic show you performed lays permanently in my eyes

Crystal blues, reds, yellows and whites color your shine

Bursts of fragments shoot out from exploding life

A captivating sight

From the farthest reaches of the night,

Your appearance is spectacular

Jung's Subject

Strong connections build between the two worlds of the mind
A conversation commences,
Able to enlighten self within a slumbered reverie
Meanings and messages unfold,
Teaching the self from inner depths of slumber

The key is provided
Yet the lock still needs to be discovered
With waking eyes, dreams replay in the brain
The ability to decipher messages from deep within
Content of dreams seamlessly travel in and out of conscience

Deep thought continues by day
Theories developed while awake and asleep
Gained knowledge from one's own mind
Psysic dreams plague my nights

The End

www.ingramcontent.com/pod-product-compliance
Lightning Source LLC
Chambersburg PA
CBHW072041060426

42449CB00010BA/2380